The Study Of Tongues

Roger Bacon

Kessinger Publishing's Rare Reprints

Thousands of Scarce and Hard-to-Find Books on These and other Subjects!

- Americana
- Ancient Mysteries
- Animals
- Anthropology
- Architecture
- Arts
- Astrology
- Bibliographies
- Biographies & Memoirs
- Body, Mind & Spirit
- Business & Investing
- Children & Young Adult
- Collectibles
- Comparative Religions
- Crafts & Hobbies
- Earth Sciences
- Education
- Ephemera
- Fiction
- Folklore
- Geography
- Health & Diet
- History
- Hobbies & Leisure
- Humor
- Illustrated Books
- Language & Culture
- Law
- Life Sciences
- Literature
- Medicine & Pharmacy
- Metaphysical
- Music
- Mystery & Crime
- Mythology
- Natural History
- Outdoor & Nature
- Philosophy
- Poetry
- Political Science
- Science
- Psychiatry & Psychology
- Reference
- Religion & Spiritualism
- Rhetoric
- Sacred Books
- Science Fiction
- Science & Technology
- Self-Help
- Social Sciences
- Symbolism
- Theatre & Drama
- Theology
- Travel & Explorations
- War & Military
- Women
- Yoga
- *Plus Much More!*

**We kindly invite you to view our catalog list at:
http://www.kessinger.net**

THIS ARTICLE WAS EXTRACTED FROM THE BOOK:

Opus Majus of Roger Bacon Part 1

BY THIS AUTHOR:

Roger Bacon

ISBN 0766126048

READ MORE ABOUT THE BOOK AT OUR WEB SITE:

http://www.kessinger.net

OR ORDER THE COMPLETE
BOOK FROM YOUR FAVORITE STORE

ISBN 0766126048

PART THREE OF THIS PLEA
On the usefulness of grammar

CHAPTER I

AFTER making the statement, therefore, that there is one perfect wisdom, which is contained in the Scriptures and must be expounded by canon law and philosophy, by which the world must be directed, nor is there needed any other science for the advantage of the human race, for it contains in itself the whole power of law and philosophy; I now wish to take up those parts of philosophy which are especially valuable for the exposition of this splendid wisdom. These are five, without which neither divine nor human things can be known, while a sure knowledge of them makes it easy for us to know all things. First, there is grammar, developed in the foreign tongues from which the wisdom of the Latins has sprung. For it is impossible for the Latins to reach what is necessary in matters divine and human except through the knowledge of other languages, nor will wisdom be perfected for them absolutely, nor relatively to the Church of God and to the remaining three matters noted above. This I now wish to state, and first with respect to absolute knowledge. For the whole sacred text has been drawn from the Greek and Hebrew, and philosophy has been derived from these sources and from Arabic: but it is impossible that the peculiar quality of one language should be preserved in another. For even dialects of the same tongue vary among different sections, as is clear from the Gallic language, which is divided into many dialects among the Gauls, Picards, Normans, Burgundians, and others. A fitting and intelligible expression in the dialect of the Picards is out of place among the Burgundians, nay, among their nearer Gallic neighbors; how much more then will this be true as between different languages? Therefore an excellent piece of work in one language cannot be transferred into another as regards the peculiar quality that it possessed in the former. Hence Jerome in his epistle on the best kind of interpretation speaks thus, "If I translate literally, the result is absurd in sound. But if any one does not think that the grace of a language is changed by translation let him translate Homer literally into Latin. I shall make a further statement; let him translate this same author in his own tongue in the words of prose, he will see a ridiculous order and a very eloquent poet speaking with difficulty." For let any one with an excellent knowledge of some science like logic or any other subject at all strive to turn this into his mother tongue, he will see that he is lacking not only in thoughts, but words, so that no one will be able to understand the science so translated as regards its potency. Therefore no Latin will be able to understand as he should the wisdom of the sacred Scripture and of philosophy, unless he understands the languages from which they were translated.

Secondly, we must consider the fact that translators did not have the words in Latin for translating scientific works, because they were not first composed in the Latin tongue. For this reason they employed very many words from other languages. Just as these words are not understood by those ignorant of those languages, so are they neither pronounced correctly nor are they written as they should be. And, what is bad, owing to their ignorance of Latin they have used Spanish, and other native tongues, to an almost endless extent in place of Latin. For let one example suffice for many from the book on Plants of Aristotle where he says, "*Belenum* which is very harmful in Persia when transplanted to Jerusalem becomes edible." This word is not the scientific one but colloquial Spanish. For *jusquiamus* [henbane] or the seed of the cassilago, is its name in Latin. After being laughed at by my Spanish students, familiar as they were with the words of their own language, when I did not understand what I was reading, I at length learned from them the meaning of this word and of many more besides.

Thirdly, although the translator ought to be perfectly acquainted with the subject which he wishes to translate and the two languages from which and into which he is translating, Boetius alone, the first translator, had full mastery of the languages; and Master Robert, called Grosse-Teste, lately bishop of Lincoln, alone knew the sciences. Certain other ordinary translators, like Girardus Cremonensis, Michael Scotus, Aluredus Anglicus, Hermannus Alemannus, whom we saw in Paris, have failed greatly as well in the languages as in the sciences; even as this same Hermannus has confessed concerning himself and others, as their translation shows. For so great is the perverseness, crudity, and terrible difficulty in the translated works of Aristotle that no one can understand them, but each one contradicts another, and false statements are found again and again, as is clear from a comparison of the different translators and of the texts of the different languages. Likewise in the sacred text false statements are found and many bad translations. For Jerome proves that the translation of the Seventy Interpreters and of Theodotion and of Aquila had many errors; and since these errors were published throughout the whole Church, and all men stood for the translation of the Seventy as for their own life, Jerome was considered a falsifier and a corrupter of the Scriptures, until little by little the truth of the Hebrew became clear when turned into Latin by the sainted Jerome. Lest, however, he should hinder the Latins by too much alteration, for this reason, as he himself writes, he sometimes adapted himself to the Seventy Interpreters, sometimes to Theodotian, sometimes to Aquila; and therefore has left much as it was translated by others, and for this reason many false statements have remained. For, as Augustine proves in the second book on Christian Doctrine, the translation given in the book of Wisdom is a bad one, "Spurious vines will not produce deep roots." For it should be, Spurious plantings, or adulterous plantings, as Augustine proves by the Greek. And yet Jerome let this pass like many other places for the peace of the Church and of the doctors. And it is clearly known that Jerome, subject to human frailty, sometimes erred in his own translation, as he himself frequently confesses. For since he had made a bad translation of the nineteenth chapter of Isaiah, he takes it up again in the original in the fifth book saying, "In this place also which we translated *curving* and *bridling* we can say *curving* and *frisking*. But while hastily translating what was written, deceived by the ambiguity we translated the Hebrew word *acmon* as *bridling*." He also again considered another place which he had translated badly in the same chapter saying, "I think it better to censure my error rather than while blushing to confess my ignorance to persist in the error. In the passage which I translated, 'and the land of Judah shall be a festivity to

Egypt,' the reading in Hebrew is *agga* which can be translated both as *festivity*, whence *aggeus* is translated as festive, and as *fear*, which Aquila has more significantly translated by *girosin*, since any one fearful and afraid turns about his eyes and fears a coming foe. Therefore if we wish to take it in a good sense that the recollection of Judah is a joy to Egypt, festivity is the right word: but if, as I judge, the idea is one of fear instead of joy we translate it terror or fear."

CHAPTER II

THE fourth reason for this condition is the fact that the Latins up to the present time lack very many philosophical and theological works. For I have seen two books of the Maccabees in Greek, namely the third and the fourth, and Scripture makes mention of the books of Samuel and Nathan and Gad the seer, and of others which we do not have. And since the whole confirmation of sacred history is given by Josephus in his books on Antiquities, and all the sacred writers take the fundamentals of their expositions from those books, it is necessary for the Latins to have that work in an uncorrupted form. But it has been proved that the Latin codices are wholly corrupt in all places on which the import of history rests, so that the text is self-contradictory everywhere. This is not the fault of so great an author, but arises from a bad translation and from the corruption by the Latins, nor can it be remedied except by a new translation or by adequate correction in all fundamental points. Likewise the books of the great doctors like the blessed Dionysius, Basil, John Chrysostom, John of Damascus, and of many others are lacking; some of which, however, Master Robert, the aforesaid bishop, has turned into Latin, and others before him translated certain other works. His work is very pleasing to theologians. If the books of these authors had been translated, not only would the learning of the Latins be augmented in a glorious way, but the Church would have stronger supports against the heresies and schisms of the Greeks, since they would be convinced by their own sacred writers whom they cannot contradict.

Likewise almost all the secrets of philosophy up to the present time lie hidden in foreign languages. For as in many instances only what is common and worthless has been translated; and much even of this character is lacking. For lines almost without number, chapters, parts of books, and whole books are omitted in the works on metaphysics, nature, logic, and on other topics, besides great secrets of the sciences and of the arts and the hidden things of nature that have not yet been translated. Such is the second philosophy of Avicenna, which he calls oriental, which is devoted to pure philosophy, and does not fear the thrusts of the lances of contradicters, and the third, conterminous with his life, in which he collected secret experiments, as he noted in the introduction to his first philosophy. Likewise, although Aristotle completed the eight principal parts of natural philosophy containing in them many sciences, we do not have all of the first part, and almost nothing of the others. And in the same way although he himself completed the nine sciences composing mathematics, we have no part of his text. What we have on metaphysics can be reckoned of no value on account of many grave defects. Although there are five great sciences composing morals, we have only the first and a little of the second. Also there is missing from his logic a book better than the others, and the book next in excellence to it has been badly translated, and cannot be known, nor is it in general use, because it has come only lately into the hands of the Latins in a defective and rough translation. Nor is it strange if I call those books of logic better, for of necessity there must be four true arguments; for two stir the speculative intellect or reason, namely, the dialectic, through the feeble and initial habit of the mind, which is opinion, so that we are disposed toward knowledge, which is the complete and final habit, in which the mind is at rest in its contemplation of truth. And this habit of the mind is acquired by the demonstrative argument. But since the will or active intellect is nobler than the theoretical and virtue united with happiness excels infinitely pure knowledge, and is without comparison more necessary for us, we must of necessity have arguments to arouse the active intellect, especially since we are weaker in this particular than in theory. For we all gladly taste of the tree of the knowledge of good and evil, but approach with difficulty the tree of life, that we may embrace the noble virtues for the sake of future felicity. Therefore the active intellect must of necessity have its own aids, and be aroused by its own proper arguments just as the speculative intellect by its arguments. And for this reason it was necessary that the teaching in regard to these arguments should be handed down, which moral philosophy and theology employ freely. For as the speculative sciences rejoice in the speculative arguments of opinion and pure knowledge, so the active sciences, as theology and active moral philosophy, consider arguments by which we are aroused to action, that is, to good works, and are turned to a love of eternal felicity. And here there are two ways of turning us. One is that which influences the mind to belief, agreement, pity, compassion, and acts of this kind; and to their contraries when there is need; and this argument is called rhetorical, and is related to the active intellect in the same way as the dialectic argument to the speculative intellect. For it causes the weak habit, namely, the persuasion of credulity and faith, to be followed by the complete habit, which is the love of what is believed and affection strengthened by opinion. And this habit, which turns us to the love of good works, is secured by the poetic argument, because true poets, like Horace and others, Greek and Latin, attack vices and magnify virtues, so as to attract men to a love of good and a hatred of sin. For as that famous poet says, "Poets wish either to benefit or please. He has won full approbation who has mingled the useful with the sweet."

For he confers no small benefit on his fellow citizens who delights them in the subject of morals. For it is necessary not only to teach, but to delight and urge forward. Hence the poet as well as the orator ought to do these three things, that by teaching he may render his hearers docile, by delighting them he may make them attentive, and by urging or turning them he may force them to work. These arguments are most potent in matters pertaining to salvation, but in purely speculative matters are impotent; just as demonstration is most effective in pure theory but wholly impotent in practical matters and in those pertaining to salvation. Accordingly Aristotle says in the first book of the Moral Philosophy that it is equally a fault for a mathematician to use a rhetorical argument and for a rhetorician to try a demonstration, since, as he says in the second book, this science does not exist for the sake of mere contemplation but for the purpose of making us good. Aristotle therefore composed books on these arguments, and Averroës and Alpharabi expounded them in their commentaries, and Avicenna instructs us in his works on logic about these arguments. Alpharabius in his book on the Sciences states that two parts of logic ought to consist of these two arguments, because logic alone ought to teach the nature of arguments and how they are composed for the use of all other sciences; and then logic serves the speculative sciences by two arguments, the dialectic and the demonstrative. Moreover, it furnishes practical arguments to morals. And because theology and canon law determine morals and laws and rights, therefore these two arguments are necessary to them, and every theologian and jurist and moral philosopher makes use of these arguments of necessity, by custom and practice, whether his plea be made to prelate, or prince, or judge, or people, or private individual, although the Latins do not yet possess the knowledge of these arguments as regards the force of the art of logic. How these arguments are composed we need not state at present; but in the work which your Beatitude has demanded they must be explained. There is nothing, however, in regard to the speculative sciences more useful in proving the faith to unbelievers, that they may be converted to a belief in the Christian faith and to a love for it; and likewise that we may be skillful preachers to all who are in need of preaching, and so also in regard to the other forms of persuasion useful for salvation. We are, moreover, greatly aided by Augustine in the third and fourth books on Christian Doctrine and by the works of Tullius and Seneca, and by their letters and certain other facts that can be collected in the Latin language concerning these arguments, although the text itself of Aristotle is lacking to us.

Chapter III

There is a fifth reason in addition, because the sciences were formed and expounded with the same idea, and therefore since the sciences were given to the Latins from other languages, all the sacred writers and Latin philosophers who expound the sciences have used copiously other languages, and multiply for us words without end in Greek, Hebrew, Chaldean, and Arabic, besides those contained in the texts. We are the sons and successors of the sacred writers and of the wise philosophers, like Boetius, Pliny, Seneca, Tullius, Varro, and other men of wisdom even up to these latest times. For we saw certain men of the past who labored much in languages, like Master Robert, mentioned above, the translator and bishop, and Thomas, the venerable president of Saint David, lately deceased, and brother Adam of Marsh, and Master Hermann, the translator, and certain other men of science. But since we do not imitate them, we therefore lack a grasp of the sciences to a degree past belief, because we cannot understand their authentic expositions and consequently we are unable to gain an understanding of the sciences. I offer two examples to serve for many. Jerome says in the prologue to his commentary on Daniel that Daniel and Esdras are written in Hebrew letters but in the Chaldean speech, also one pericope of Jeremiah. Now all theologians state that this pericope consists of the Lamentations of Jeremiah, because pericope is the same as small part. But all Hebrews know that the Lamentations are written in Hebrew letters and in the speech of the Hebrews. Any one who knows anything about Hebrew can perceive this; hence the boy here is not ignorant of this fact. Then we can mention this pericope from the tenth chapter of Jeremiah, where it is said, "Thus therefore shall ye say unto them, Let the Gods that have not made the heavens and the earth perish from the earth and from those things which are under the heavens." For this passage alone in Jeremiah is written in the Chaldean language, as all Hebrew scholars know. It is certain that the Chaldean and the Hebrew have the same tongue but a different dialect, like the Gaul and the Picard; for dialect is the particular form of a language determined by a nation. Hence the Hebrew says *Heloim* for God or Gods, the Chaldean says *Heloa,* and for heaven or heavens the Hebrew says *Samaim,* the Chaldean *Samaa,* and for *not* the Hebrew says *lo,* but the Chaldean *la;* and thus there are accidental differences in the same language. Such is the case in the pericope mentioned above. Yet before this pericope is written here in Hebrew and Chaldean, the Hebrew alphabet must be given in order that the subject under discussion may be more easily understood. The letters of the

Study of Tongues

Hebrew alphabet are written first, then in the line above are given their names, and last our letters corresponding to the Hebrew ones, in order that we may know the value of the letters and the sounds indicated, some being vowels and some consonants.

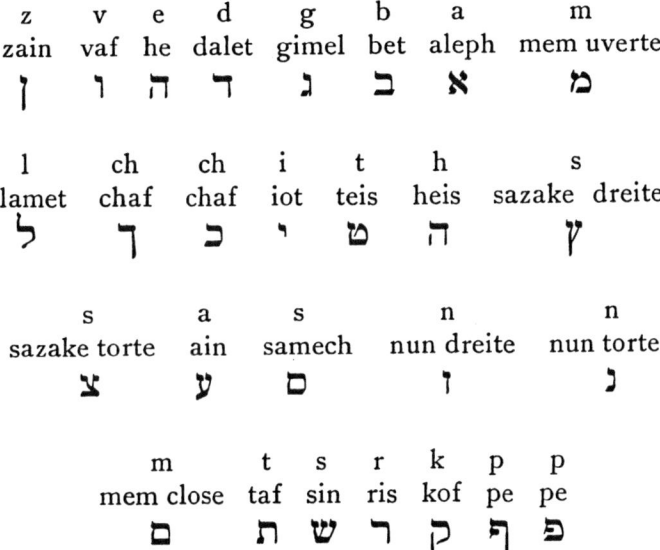

There are six vowels, *aleph, ain, he, heth, iot, vav;* the rest are consonants; *he* and *heth* are aspirated, *he* at the beginning, *heth* not only at the beginning, but at the end, and *heth* is produced in the throat, *he* in the mouth. *Aleph* likewise in the mouth and *ain* in the throat. But we must bear in mind that *iot* has only one sound, namely, j, like our j, and becomes a consonant and vowel like j with us. V, as Jerome says in his Hebrew Questions, has a double sound, namely our v and o. The remaining four have the sound of our five vowels, namely, a, e, i, o, u, as is shown by Jerome in the book of interpretations. This difference of sounds they indicate by points and dashes. For if under *aleph* a line be drawn without a point thus, א or with a point under the line thus, אֲ, the sound is a. But if two points are made lying under the *aleph* crosswise, אֱ, or two vertically, אֳ, or three like a triangle, אֶ, or five points in this way, אֵ, the sound is e. But if

Opus Majus

three points lying under *aleph* descend obliquely thus, אֻ, the sound is u. If one point be placed under the letter, אִ, the sound is i. But if a point be placed above it, the sound is o, thus, אֹ. The same is true of *ain* and *he* and *heth,* which have these five sounds by means of difference in pointing. When *vaf* has the sound of u, there may be the sign of the three points, as stated, thus, וֻ, or one point may be placed in its bosom thus, וּ. The letters for the vowels are not often written, but the vowel signs mentioned above take their place. Therefore we must note that they attach these signs to the consonants to indicate what vowel sound is to be joined in the syllable with the consonant. If I wish to indicate *ba, be, bi, bo, bu,* I must write,

ba	be	bi	bo	bu
בַּ	בֶּ	בִּ	בֹּ	בֻּ

There are likewise other signs indicating strengthened or weakened sounds of the consonants. Hence when a dash is placed above the letter it is weakened; when a point is placed in its bosom the letter is strengthened. Hence when a dash is placed above *daleth* thus, ד̄, a weakened sound is indicated like our z, as when I say, *adamas.* But when a point is placed in its bosom thus, דּ, the sound is strengthened, as when I say, *dabo.* And thus we here find in this Hebrew which follows

sic	dicetis	eis	dii
chidena	temerun	lehom	elaa
כִּדְנָה	תֵּאמְרוּן	לְהוֹם	אֱלָהַיָּא

Hebrew letters / Chaldean tongue

qui	coelum	terram et	non
di	semaa	areka ve	la
דִּי	שְׁמַיָּא	וְאַרְקָא	לָא

fecerunt	pereant	terra de
ebadu	iebedu	area me
עֲבַדוּ	יֵאבַדוּ	מֵאַרְעָא

Study of Tongues

	coelo		sub de et
	semaa		thehot mi u
	שְׁמַיָּא׃		וּסְתָחוֹת

dii	eis	dicetis	sic	
elohim	lahem	tomeru	co	) Hebrew letters
אֱלֹהִים	לָהֶם	תֹּאמְרוּ	כֹּה	) Hebrew tongue

fecerunt	non	terram et	coelum	qui
asu	lo	ares ve	samaim	eser
עֲשׂוּ	לֹא	וְאָרֶץ	שָׁמַיִם	אֲשֶׁר

sub de et	terra de	pereant
thahat mi u	eres me	iobedu
וּמִתַּחַת	מֵאֶרַע	יֹאבְדוּ

isto	coelo
ele	samaim
אֵלֶּה׃	שָׁמַיִם

There is therefore a manifest and wretched error on the part of all in this matter owing to ignorance of these languages. Another example is taken from Greek. Since many Greek examples will be given in what follows, I wish for this reason to give here the Greek alphabet with the diphthongs which they use in writing: for what I have to say will be made clearer by this means.

a	b	g	d	e		
alpha	vita	gamma	delta	e. penti, *i.e.* quintum		
α	β	γ	δ	ε		

z	i	th	i	k	l	m	n
zita	ita	thita	iota	kappa	labda	mi	ni
ζ	η	θ	ι	κ	λ	μ	ν

Opus Majus

x	o	p	r	s	t
xi	o. micron	pi	ro	sima	taf
ξ	o	π	ρ	σ	τ

y. Greek among Latins	ph	ch	ps
y. psilo	phi	chi	psi
υ	φ	χ	ψ

o
o.mega, *i.e.* magnum
ω

There are seven vowels, counting the different letters, since there is a threefold i and a twofold o. But there are only four vowels possessing a principal sound, namely, a, e, i, o. The diphthong with the Greeks is a union of two vowels with the sound of one, or a vowel with a consonant; and the final letters in the diphthongs of the Greeks are *iota* and *ipsilo*. *Ipsilo* therefore can follow *alpha* thus, αυ, and then the sound is like a with υ consonantal, a sound somewhat similar to the sound of a itself with f, and therefore we commonly explain the sound as that of *af;* or it can follow e thus, ευ, and then the sound is like e vocal with υ consonant, and like *ef,* as was stated in regard to *alpha* and *ipsilo;* or it can follow *ita* thus, ηυ, and sounds like *if,* as was stated concerning the others; or *ipsilo* can follow *o micron* thus, ου, and then it has the vowel sound of u; and in this case only do the Greeks have the sound of this vocal u. If *iota* follows *alpha* thus, αι, then the sound is e; if it follows e thus, ει , then the sound is i through the *iota;* if it follows o thus, οι, it has the y sound through the *ipsilo*. It can also follow *ypsilo* itself, thus, υι, and then it has the i sound with the *ipsilo*. These eight diphthongs are called proper diphthongs. But three are called improper, and are made by writing this letter *iota* beneath *alpha, ita,* and ω *mega,* thus, ᾳ, ῃ, ῳ. Sometimes, however, *iota* is placed on the line after the letter as in other diphthongs, thus, αι, but in improper diphthongs the sound never alters, but remains that of the principal letter, that is, of the letter beneath which the *iota* is written. For when it is written beneath *alpha,* the sound is a; when beneath *ita,* the sound is *ita;* when beneath ω *mega,* only the ω *mega* sounds.

Study of Tongues

The Greeks use these three diphthongs always in the dative case of the first and second declensions.

Now the example in the present instance is concerning Jacob, who meeting his brother Esau coming from Mesopotamia said, "For thus I beheld thy face, as the face of God." Augustine asks in the book of Questions, and it is in the gloss, how a holy man could compare an evil one to God and reckon him as God. He answers the question with the statement that the word God is used in Scripture in many ways, sometimes for the true God and sometimes otherwise; but the Seventy Translators, in order to point out that he was not speaking of the true God, added the article to the name of God. For the article has the property of showing the truth of a thing; but this force does not appear in Latin, since it lacks the article. But it does appear in the Gallic tongue; and hence when they say in Paris, *li reis vient,* the article *li* designates the particular and actual king of such a place, since they are speaking of the king of France. This would not suffice to denote the arrival of the English king to the city of Paris. For no one would say of the English king's coming to Paris, *li reis vient,* but would add something, *li reis de Engleterre vient.* Therefore the article alone suffices to designate the truth and property of the thing under discussion. For this reason Augustine says that the Greek runs thus, προσωπον θεου, which in Greek has the sound *prosopon theu* without the article; and not thus, προσωπον του θεου. *Prosopon* here signifies countenance or face, *theu* is the genitive case of this noun *theos,* that is, God, and *tu* is the article in the genitive. There is great need, therefore, that the Latins should know languages on account of the sayings of the sacred writers and of other men of science.

Chapter IV

The sixth reason is the correction of errors and false statements without end in the text of theology as well as philosophy, not only in the letter, but in the sense. That, moreover, correction is necessary I prove by the great amount of corruption. Since the error in the text of God is more serious and dangerous than in the text of philosophy, I shall therefore apply the power of languages to the corruption of the sacred text, that the necessity of these may appear, owing to the endless corruption of the edition in common use, that of Paris. God knows that nothing can be brought before the Apostolic Seat in need of such vigorous correction as this endless corruption. For the letter in the common text is everywhere false or in doubt for the man who has taken this corruption into account, and if the letter be false or in doubt, then the sense, spiritual as well as literal, will contain falsehood and inexpressible doubt. This I now wish to show without possible contradiction. For Augustine says against Faustus, "If there is disagreement in the Latin codices, we must have recourse to the ancient ones and to several of them." For the ancient ones, as he thinks, are to be preferred to the late ones, and the larger number to the fewer. But all the ancient Bibles, which lie everywhere in the monasteries, and which up to the present time have not been glossed nor touched, have the true translation, which the holy Roman Church received in the beginning, and ordered spread abroad throughout all the churches.

But there are many contradictions in the edition of Paris. Therefore this edition needs a thorough correction by means of the ancient texts. But Augustine says in the same work that if a doubt still remains in the ancient Bibles, we must then have recourse to the Hebrew and Greek languages. He also makes this statement in the second book on Christian Doctrine, and shows it in examples. Jerome also imparts this teaching to Frecella and Sunnia and so states in the commentary on Zachariah, and all the sacred writers agree in this, and any one else with reason. But Greek and Hebrew along with the ancient Bibles stand in opposition to the Paris edition, and hence it is in need of correction in many places. But Jerome says to Damasus in this event that where there is diversity, the truth is not known. But those who are striving with all the truth they know to correct the text, namely, the two orders of Dominicans and Franciscans, have now formed from the corrupted text various scriptures and more than one Bible may contain. They contend with each other and contradict without end; and not only the orders, but the brothers of both orders, oppose one another even more than the orders as a whole. For every house contradicts another, and in the same house correctors succeeding one another in

CLEMENT IV

From *Effigies Pontificum Romanorum Dominici Basae*

turn destroy their mutual positions with infinite scandal and confusion. Hence although twenty years before Dominicans effected a correction in the Scriptures, others have come and arranged a new correction, which contains more than the half of one Bible, some of whose flowers when collected are scarcely contained in so great a space as that required for the New Testament. And because they see that they have erred in the old correction, they have now made a statute that no one shall adhere to it, and yet the second correction on account of its dreadful length has along with many truths incomparably more false statements than the first correction, as your Glory will be able clearly to perceive when the proof in particular shall be presented to your authority.

CHAPTER V

WHAT I have shown in general can be shown in examples. For corruption of the text takes place without limit by the addition, substraction, alteration, union, division of statement, word, syllable, letter, diphthong, mark of breathing, so that not only the letter but the literal and spiritual sense is changed. The faults are found not only in one statement, but in many, nay, they affect many folios. I shall now give one or two examples of each of these faults. For many prologues are placed in the text superfluously, since they are not prologues of the text giving an explanation of the translation of the books to which they are prefixed; but they are either letters sent to friends, like the letter of Jerome to Paul, which in the caption of the Bible is reckoned a prologue and is commonly so called, and yet it is contained in the book of Jerome's epistles; or they are prologues to commentaries on originals not to the text, like the one prefixed to the book of Ecclesiastes. For without doubt it is the prologue of the original itself and this is clear from its purport. And the same is true of many others which are not in ancient Bibles. Of a superfluous statement there is an example in Deuteronomy, "Cursed be he that sleepeth with the wife of his neighbor, and the people shall say Amen"; since neither the ancient codices nor the Hebrew or Greek have this verse. Of a superfluous word there is a horrible and dreadful example in the eighth chapter of Genesis, when the statement is made that the raven did not return to the ark. For the Hebrew has the affirmative and all the Jews hold this view: and the ancient Bibles have the affirmative, and Jerome in the original. The negative was accepted a short time after from another translation, doubtless that of the Seventy, whose falseness Jerome shows in numberless places, and which since the time of Isidore and before has been discredited. For he himself states in his book on the Offices that as a general rule all Latin Churches use the translation of Jerome, because it is more truthful in the expression of thought and clearer in phraseology, with the exception that owing to the frequent practice of singing in the Church the translation of the Psalter following the Septuagint has remained. But before the Roman Church ordered this translation to be used everywhere, Augustine and others and Jerome himself in his time used, as did the Church, the ancient translation. Therefore when Augustine quotes this text in the sixteenth book of the City of God and expounds it, he had to use the translation in common use and received among the Latins, nor could he do otherwise. Since, indeed, a glossarist a hundred years later placed glosses on the text, he accepted the authority of Augustine from the City of God, and placed the negative beside the text, but he did not alter the text nor did he insert the negative. Modern scribes, paying no attention to the difference in translations, nor considering what translation they were using, have inserted the negative on their own authority and in the first instance some one noted among the rest did this. In this way a terrible error was spread abroad, since a contradiction is given for its opposite. But we see in philosophy that there is sometimes a double or triple translation of the same book, and one translation has what is different from another or sometimes what is contrary. But there is no one who has ventured to mix one translation with another.

The error found in ecclesiastical books of reading a negative was introduced by those interested in these books from a corruption of the original. As regards the change of a syllable, and consequently of the whole word, there is a strange example in the case of Joseph, who is said in the common version to have been sold for thirty pieces of silver on account of the example of the Lord. But according to the ancient codices, and the Hebrew,

Study of Tongues

Greek, Arabic, and Jerome in the original, and Josephus in the first book on Antiquities, the reading should be twenty, not thirty. Likewise in the Psalter by a change of syllable the whole word is changed with great error, when it reads, "My soul has thirsted for God the living fountain." For since the Church uses the translation of the Seventy in the Psalter alone, Jerome has corrected this translation twice, and has placed *fortem* where we put *fontem* through an error due to the similarity of the words, and because in the preceding verse mention is made of fountain, and because thirst corresponds to the idea of water. But as I have said, Jerome has corrected it to *fortem;* and this is the reading in the Hebrew and the Greek, and in Jerome's own translation which he made from the Hebrew. This is also the reading in all ancient Bibles, and in the ancient Psalters of the monasteries. For I have examined this matter carefully, and there is assuredly here merely a very despicable error due to the similarity mentioned.

As regards the change of a letter this a notable example in the first chapter of Judges where we find the words *in monte Hares*. *Hares* is interpreted by *testateo* [of tile, or brick], with the penult letter e not i; but it is generally taken as *testatio* with an i, so that it would be a nominative case and formed like *testificatio* from *teste;* but it must be the ablative derived from *testa,* for in all ancient books it is *testateo* with an e, both in Greek and Hebrew, when *Hares* occurs. Jerome has translated it by tile, or by something derived from tile, or by something like it, as brick or dryness. For *Hares* in Hebrew signifies tile or some one of the aforesaid meanings in Latin. Hence Jerome in the sixth book on Isaiah expounding this word in the sixteenth chapter, "To those who rejoice over walls of baked brick," says, "*Hares* signifies tile or baked brick," and in the eighth book, expounding this word in the twenty-fourth chapter of Isaiah, "The moon grows red," he says that *Hares* signifies tile or dryness. The fact that in the thirty-first and thirty-second chapters of Jeremiah the names *Ananeel* and *Anameel* are erroneously confounded, so that the letters m and n are placed without distinction in the penult, is a great error in the change of one letter. For Jerome says in the original that *Ananeel* written with an n is a tower, with an m is the son of Sellum, cousin on the father's side of Jeremiah; and it is so found in the Hebrew.

As regards the diphthong, there is that example in the sixteenth chapter of Proverbs, *lapides sacculi* [stones of the bag] according to the Hebrew and the Greek and ancient writers, although it is commonly given as *seculi* without a diphthong for *saeculi* in some not very ancient writers. The error in this instance secured a foothold because this noun *seculum* ought to be written with the diphthong, and it is thus correctly written in all ancient books in every instance. Since there is only a slight difference between c and e, some of the old writers of our own times were deceived and changed the first c into an e, thus writing *saeculi;* and since modern writers do not write it with a diphthong, they have therefore retained this noun *seculum* written in their own way, and have neglected the noun *sacculum*, which has the correct letter.

As to the mark of breathing there is an example in the First Epistle to the Thessalonians, when we read, *"Ad tempus ore,"* so that *ore* would be the ablative case of this noun *os oris*, and not the genitive of this noun *hora horae*. It is written therefore in the ablative case, and is glossed, not by a sacred writer, but by the Master of Sentences, who glossed the Epistles; but just as he has failed in many instances elsewhere owing to his ignorance of Greek, so has he failed here, since without question in Greek from which it was taken the genitive case of this noun *hora* is found to be *horas* and is aspirated in both Greek and Latin. But *os oris* is not aspirated, for this noun *hora* is Greek, although it is declined in the Latin manner like *domina*. But Greek declines it thus, *hora, horas, hora, horan, hora.* Hence the nominative, dative, and vocative are alike, the accusative in *an,* genitive in *as;* ablative the Greeks do not have. And this word in the Greek is *horas,* as I have read with care, and any one can prove it who knows Greek, and the aspirate is found in ancient writers.

I have desired to offer these examples, that some proof may be given by way of hint of the necessity of knowing foreign languages, owing to the corruption of the Latin text both in theology and in philosophy. But the method followed in a clear proof, and particularly in one dealing with all the corruptions of the Bible, is postponed to another time, owing to the greatness of the matter, which can, when you wish so to order, be presented to your Holiness, but not by me adequately but rather by another; the importance of which I shall explain to you in what follows.

Chapter VI

THE seventh reason why it is necessary that the Latins should know languages is particularly false interpretation, although the text be absolutely correct. For in both theology and philosophy interpretations are necessary, especially so in the sacred text and in the text of medicine and in that of the secret sciences, which are too obscure owing to the ignorance of interpretations. For physicians are confused because of the bad interpretations which they call synonyma. For it is not possible for them to use the established remedies owing to the error in these synonyma, and therefore there is no end of peril in their hands. It is the same with the sacred text; for the chief difficulty in knowing it is due to the variety and obscurity of an infinite number of interpretations, as is clear in a familiar example which will serve for others without number. For the common interpretation of the name Israel for the patriarch is the "man beholding God," and this continued in use up to the time of Jerome, and even up to the time that his translation and exposition were ordered to be used in all the churches. But he himself says in the original, although they are men of great influence, who have interpreted Israel as the "man beholding God," and although their shadow oppresses us, yet we agree with God rather, or the angel who gave this name, than with the authority of a man of secular eloquence. He accordingly proves his assertion in admirable fashion. For those who interpreted it thus believed that this word has the same signification united as when divided, like *respublica* with us. But this is not in general true, nay, there is an instance of it in many cases in every tongue. Now in Hebrew *is* is man, *ra* beholding, *el* God, and therefore they believed that this name of the patriarch must be divided into those three words. But Jerome proves this interpretation false by many arguments; for four arguments can be drawn from his statements based on the word, and four or five based on the fact. For in those three words there are other letters and more in number than in the name of the patriarch and they are found in a different order and syllabication. Therefore from this triple argument taken from the letters Jerome concludes that there cannot be the same signification in this case and in that; since the reason for the same signification rests on the identity of the words. But it is clear that the word and the letters differ too much, since in the name of the patriarch there are these five letters in order, *iod, sin, res, aleph, lamet,* as the Hebrew thus arranged shows יִשְׂרָאֵל, Iserael. But in this triple word these eight letters have the following order, *aleph, iod, sin, res, aleph, he, aleph, lamet,* as the Hebrew shows.

is	ra	el
אִישׁ	רָאָה	אֵל

A fourth argument can be drawn from the pronunciation. For, as the points show, the proper name does not retain in the Hebrew the exact sound of those three words, but it has a greater sound, because Iserael is pronounced in four syllables; but the three words are limited in pronunciation to only three syllables, so that we say *is, ra, el;* since one point under a letter has the sound of *i*, two points that of *e*, and a line with a point beneath it has the sound of *a*. But according to Jerome stronger arguments are drawn from the sense of the word. For it is shown by the text, Hebrew, Greek, and Latin, and by Josephus that Israel ought not to be called "the man beholding God," but "chief or prince with God," since in Hebrew the literal sense is as follows, "And God said, thy name shall be called no more Jacob, but Israel, since if thou wast a chief or prince with God, thou shall be able to be one with men also." Therefore Jerome says that the sense is, "Thy name shall not be supplanter, that is Jacob, but thy name shall be prince with God, that is Israel. For since I am a prince, so shalt thou be called a prince who wast able to wrestle with me. If moreover thou wast able to strive with me, how much more with men, that is with Esau, whom thou shouldst not fear." And the Hebrew itself shows this here written in this way.

Study of Tongues

Jacob	non	dixit et
iaecove	lo	iomer va
יַעֲקֹב	לֹא	וַיֹּאמֶר

nomen tuum	amodo	dicetur
simecha	oze	ieamer
שִׁמְךָ	עוֹד	יֵאָמֵר

quoniam	Israel	si	quoniam
ki	icerael	im	ki
כִּי	יִשְׂרָאֵל	אִם	כִּי

Deo	simul	principatus
elohim	im	saritha
אֱלֹהִים	עִם	שָׂרִיתָ

poteris et	hominibus	simul et
tuchal va	enasime	im ve
וַתּוּכָל	אֲנָשִׁים	וְעִם

The Greek text has the verse as follows: "Since thou didst prevail with God, with men also shalt thou be strong." And the Latin has: "Since thou wast strong against God, how much more wilt thou prevail against men." Josephus in the first book of the Antiquities says that he was called Israel because he withstood an angel. Therefore all these expressions, namely, to be a prince with God, and to prevail, and to be strong, and to stand against or with God, are reduced to the same meaning, as is evident, but interpreted by different words, no one of which in virtue of its meaning can have the signification of beholding God. Therefore the true interpretation is "a prince with God." And in addition Jerome confirms this by an argument from derivation. For Sarith, which is derived from the name Israel, means prince, as he states. Whence also Sara the wife of Abraham is called princess, just as Jerome says on the seventeenth chapter of Genesis. Wherefore if people in general or some ancient writers, like Eusebius of Caesarea in his book of Hebrew Names, which Jerome translated into Latin, and others, abusing a well-known interpretation, say that Israel is interpreted as the "man beholding God," we may say with Jerome: "The interpretation of Israel as *the man beholding God*, given in the book of Names and generally accepted seems to be more forced than true." If, therefore, any one should argue that his authorities for the statement that the true meaning of this word Israel is "the man beholding God" are Eusebius in the book of Names, translated by Jerome into Latin, and Ambrose and other perchance sacred writers, we must answer that they spoke following the common exposition, before the truth was disclosed, which later the blessed Jerome revealed to the Latins by a true and correct interpretation; even as it is contained in his books, and appears also in the gloss. If, therefore, it be said that it is the custom of modern theologians to take this interpretation, the proper answer is indicated in the statements given above of Augustine, Cyprian, Isidore, and others. For according to them custom should yield to truth when revealed, in order that giving up the error of the throng we may follow the truth; and that which has come from ignorance ought not to be alleged in proof, as is being done in the matter under discussion. And above all we should not oppose a sacred author and teacher when he brings forward in support of his position convincing reasons and authorities. Furthermore, for the assurance of all, any one can consult Hebrew scholars, and he will find the judgment of the blessed Jerome ratified and unshaken. There is the greatest need of remedies against false statement in these interpretations on account of the form of Hebrew speech. For in the common interpretations, which are placed at the end of the Bible, there are infinite occasions for errors because a word is reckoned according to the Latin standard which has many forms in Hebrew. And there is the greater error because to such a word various interpretations are given, as though they belonged to the same Hebrew word, whereas each belongs to a different one, because a Hebrew word written by us without due consideration in a single way has different letters in Hebrew and different ways of writing, according to which it receives different meanings. Jerome gives an example

Study of Tongues

of this in his epistle on Mansions.* For *or,* if it is written with *aleph,* means light; if with *ain,* skin; with *heth,* hole; with *he,* mountain. He says, therefore, that in the twentieth chapter of Numbers some have interpreted it in these four ways; but he eliminates three of these because in the Hebrew this word is written with the letter *he,* and therefore in this place has the meaning of mountain only. But in preaching and reading theologians have recourse to all four expositions in this word; and so also in other words because of their various interpretations.

The last scientific reason for the need of other languages is the fact that Latin grammar was formed from Greek and Hebrew. For we received our letters from the Greeks, as Priscianus shows, and the whole method of treating the parts of speech Priscianus received from the Greeks, as he bears witness, and he mixes Greek freely in all his books. The words themselves of the Latin tongue, both theological and philosophical, were brought in for the most part from other languages; of which words the Latins suspect some to be from another tongue, while others they do not consider as descending from such a source. Many, in fact, are reckoned as wholly Latin when in reality they are Greek or Hebrew, Arabic or Chaldean, in which words error is frequent on the part of the Latins in their pronunciation, writing, and meaning. For it is no small impropriety to make mistakes in words; because as a consequence a man errs in his statements, then in his arguments, and at length in what he reckons as conclusions. For Aristotle says, "Those who are ignorant of the meaning of words often reason falsely." Boetius places the first and principal foundation of learning in an exact and complete knowledge of terms, as he shows in his work Disciplina Scholarium; and we experience this in each of the sciences. For the principal difficulty in a science and its usefulness are found in knowing how to understand the words employed in the science, and to express them in a wise manner and without error. When a man has advanced thus far, he can accomplish the rest by himself without further teaching if he be diligent in study. For the texts of the sciences are plain to him after he has learned how properly and correctly to understand and interpret; and without difficulty he can understand any scientist, and can confer ably with any one, and be instructed,

* *I.e.,* the forty-two stopping-places of the Children of Israel.

if necessary, by any one. Aristotle says in the first book of the Heavens and the World, "A small error in fundamentals is a great one in what is derived from them." For he who makes an error in the foundation of necessity piles up his whole building on the error.

We judge, therefore, that our language is composed of Latin words and contains few words from other tongues, whereas words in common use are from foreign tongues, as *domus, scyphus, clericus, laicus, diabolus, Sathanas, ego, pater, mater, ambo, leo, bos, ager, malum,* and a host of others which with difficulty could be contained in a large volume; especially so if the words used in the different sciences were examined, particularly theology and medicine. Nothing would be more useful than such a volume, if it furnished all the words correctly written and properly pronounced, together with a trustworthy derivation and an accurate interpretation. But as it is we make countless mistakes in these four particulars to the great detriment of all learning, as we can perceive from a few examples. For we do not consider the order of languages, nor the fact that an earlier language does not receive the interpretation of a later one, nor that different languages in that in which they are different do not mutually expound themselves, as Jerome says on the seventeenth chapter of Genesis, "No one in naming a thing in one language takes the etymology of the word from another." Servius also makes this statement in the commentaries on Vergil. Above all, an earlier language cannot have its origin in a later one, as is clear to every reasonable man. Hence Greek does not spring from Latin, nor Hebrew from Greek. Therefore Hebrew must not take its etymology from Greek, nor Greek from Latin. Hence Jerome says in the place mentioned, replying to certain objectors, "*Sarra* ought not to have an explanation from the Greek but from the Hebrew, since it is a Hebrew word." Servius says that *Lenaeus* is derived from *lenos*, wine vat, not from *lenio*, because a Greek noun cannot have a Latin etymology. But we commonly and without distinction disregard this rule. For we say that *amen*, although it is Hebrew, is derived from *a*, the Greek prefix, meaning without, and *mene* a Greek word meaning defection. And although *Parasceve* is Greek, we say that it is derived from *paro, paras,* and *coena, coenae,* which are Latin words.

Study of Tongues

The statement is also made that *dogma* is derived from *doceo*, and that *jubileum* comes from *jubilo*, and similarly in regard to a host of other words, all of which derivations are false. Not only the rank and file of the Latins but the authorities err in these matters; as, for example, Hugutio and his followers, who think that *jubileum* is derived from *jubilo*, whereas *jubileum* must be Hebrew and *jubilus* is Latin. But the word should not be written *jubileum* with the letter *i* in the second syllable as in *jubilo;* but it should have the letter *e* and be written *jubeleus*, as Isidore and Papias maintain, and all ancient books so have it. For it is derived from *jobel*, which is Hebrew.

Chapter VII

Since, moreover, we know that many words in use among Latins must be interpreted through other tongues, we believe, owing to our familiarity with this fact, that far more words than the fact warrants derive their etymology from a foreign source. For only those words having a Greek and a Hebrew origin and derivation ought to be interpreted by those languages. For words of pure Latin origin can have no exposition except by means of Latin words. For the pure Latin is altogether different from every other tongue, and therefore does not have an interpretation from a foreign source. But the Latins pay no attention to this fact, nay, without distinction they interpret pure Latin words by other languages, like the words derived from the Greeks. Hence in many ways they interpret in Greek this word *caelum,* which is pure Latin, stating that *caelum* is equivalent to *casa helios,* that is, house of the sun, for the sun is called *helios.* But their statement is inconsistent and false. For since *helios* is in the nominative case and not in the genitive, *casa helios* is inconsistent; for they should say *casa heliu,* because *heliu* is in the genitive case. Secondly, the statement is false; for as Varro, most learned of the Latins, to quote the words of sacred writers and philosophers, teaches us, and Pliny confirms his statement in the prologue to his Natural Philosophy, that *caelum* is derived from *caelo, caelas,* that is, *sculpo-pis,* because it is carved and adorned with stars, which is manifest from the rule for writing words. For *caelo-las* for *sculpo-pis* is written with the diphthong *ae* in all ancient books; and likewise this noun *caelum* in all the ancient codices is written with this same diphthong, and is therefore derived from *caelo*, which is the same as *sculpo*. Hence it follows that it is not derived from *celo, celas*, which is a synonym for *occulto-tas*, as those claim who give this noun a Latin etymology, stating that it is so called because it is hidden and far removed from us. These interpreters like those preceding have been deceived by a wretched error. Likewise this word *ave*, which is pure Latin, they expound in Greek, stating that it is formed from *a*, meaning without, and *ue*, as though it were *sine ue*. But this cannot be since this word is not taken from the Greek word of cognate signification. For *chere* in Greek signifies *ave* in Latin, but these two words do not agree, and therefore much less will it draw its exposition from other sources. This then is one way in which mistakes are made in an almost countless number of Latin words.

Chapter VIII

ANOTHER form of error is due to the fact that we do not pay attention to the many different ways of writing in Greek words, and that words very similar in sound are distinguished in meaning. The Greeks have three forms of *i*, two of *o* and two of *t, p*, and *c*; they have eleven diphthongs and many other ways of showing the variation of their words in meaning. For *cenos*, meaning empty, from which comes *cenodoxia*, that is, vanity, of which we read in the seventh chapter of Deuteronomy, is written with a short *e*; and *cenos*, that is, new, from which comes *encenia*, that is, innovations like a new feast and dedications of churches, of which we read in the tenth chapter of John, is written with the diphthong *ae*, thus, *caenos*. But *cenos*, that is, common, from which come *cenobium* and *epicenon*, is written with the diphthong *oi*, although the Latin has an *e*, but it should have *i*, so as to read *cinos*. Hence from this word is formed *cinomia*, which is, according to Jerome in his correction of the Psalter, the common fly or fly of every kind. Hence Papias says that it is written with the diphthong in the first syllable thus, *coinomia*, and this is proved from the Greek

Psalter. Also the word *cynos,* dog, when it is written with the Greek *y,* whence *cynomia,* that is, dog fly, of which we read in the eighth chapter of Exodus. The word *xenos* with *x* means foreign, from which comes *xenia,* meaning presents or gifts, of which we read in the first book of Maccabees and in the twentieth chapter of Ecclesiasticus. Also *schenos* with *sch* is a rope, from which is formed *schenobates,* one who walks on a rope or over a rope; and *scena* means shade or tent, from which is formed *scenopegia,* that is, setting up a tent or the art of tent-making, at which Paul the Apostle labored. Since, therefore, the derivatives and compounds of those words differ so in their meanings, although they are similar in expression and sound, like the words from which they are derived, it is clear that he cannot escape error in the literal sense who disregards the written form of words of this kind. Hence many famous living expositors have been at times deceived, such as Rabanus, who on the eighteenth chapter of the Acts says that the *schenofactoria ars* [art of tent-making] teaches how to make ropes, because he thought that *schenos* meaning rope is the word from which the noun is derived. But Bede teaches to the contrary, holding that it is derived from *scena* [tent]. And this is shown clearly in the writing of the word, namely, in the eighteenth chapter of the Acts, in the Greek text the word is written with the first syllable lacking the aspirate, and with the vowel called *ita,* that is long *i,* and is so written *scena* for tent; but *schenos,* meaning rope, is written with the diphthong *oe,* and with the aspirate. And thus there is a contention among the doctors about *cynomia* and the other words mentioned. Hence as regards *xenia* the majority believes that it does not exist and corrects it in the sacred text into *exenia.* But in the ancient Bibles it is not so written, nor in Greek, nor can the word be so formed according to Greek grammar, because it would require the placing there of the Greek preposition *ex,* which is impossible, since the word begins with a consonant, as is clear according to the grammar of the Greeks. In this way error arises in almost countless words.

Opus Majus

Chapter IX

THE third form of error is due to the fact that we do not observe as we should that while the Latins have much in common with the Greeks they yet differ from them in some particulars. For since Priscianus states the fact and all the Latins are aware that the name of a tree is in the feminine gender and terminates in *us,* and the name of a fruit is neuter and terminates in *um,* as *pomus, pomum; pirus, pirum,* etc., they think that this principle holds good in regard to all words in use among the Latins, like the words *malum* and *amigdalum* and others. For the Latin rule is to be understood as applying only to Latin words, not to Greek words nor to others. That this is a fact is clear in the first place because the Latin gives its rules concerning Latin words, and it is not within its province to form rules for other languages; in the second place, Priscianus says that every Greek word passing into Latin retains its own gender that it had in Greek; and therefore since the word *malum* for tree is Greek and of neuter gender, it will remain so in Latin; and therefore whether it has the meaning of fruit or of tree it will be of the same gender and of the same termination. And this is proved by Vergil, who says in the Georgics *mala insita;* trees are ingrafted, not fruits; and in regard to this Servius the commentator, who was greater than Priscianus, for he frequently quotes the authority of Servius, says that this rule, "All names of trees are feminine," is to be understood of Latin, not of Greek nouns. The word *malum,* moreover, is Greek, as he states; and it is certain that it is Greek, although in accordance with Latin custom pronounced somewhat differently, since no word in Greek ends in the letter m, but in n; and Latin is accustomed to terminate its own words in m, as *scamnum, lignum, pomum,* and the like. Likewise the Latin often changes a vowel in a Greek word, as where the Greek says *grammaticos* the Latin has *grammaticus,* and so in many instances. This is the case here, for the Greek says *melon* for tree and fruit; the Latin changes the e into a, and n into m, and says *malum.* But this change does not alter the word as regards the nature and root; because it was taken from Greek, although altered in pronunciation, and to this fact all authorities bear witness. But throughout Latin texts in ancient books on theology and philosophy we always find the word *malum* for tree. For in the first chapter of Joel *malum* for tree is generally found in all Bibles; and up to the present time the correctors have let it pass in the new Bibles, and in all the ancient Bibles it is likewise found in the fourth chapter of Canticles, where we read, "As the appletree among the trees of the wood"; and so Bede expounds it in the original. And in the twelfth chapter of Ecclesiastes is the word *amigdalum* in all ancient Bibles; and *malogranatum* in the singular and *malogranata* in the plural are found in the books of the law, which would not happen if *malum* were not of the neuter gender. Therefore these words are changed in accordance with the form of Latin words inconsistently, and it is particularly strange that in one passage the correctors allow the ancient letter to remain, and in another passage rub it out, a procedure altogether opposed to reason.

Chapter X

LIKEWISE in the pronunciation of the Greek letters there is a great deal of error because the Latins wish to keep their own manner of pronunciation in the Greek words. And in this there is a very grave error; since all the Latin poets and all the ancient Latins pronounced according to the primitive custom. But we of modern times have violated this rule in many ways contrary to the practice of all the ancient Latins and their authors. For example, when Priscianus says that possessive adjectives ending in *nus* are long and are accented on the penult, as *Latinus, bovinus, equinus,* and the like, the rule is to be understood of Latin words, not of Greek, for certain reasons previously touched upon. And therefore since *adamantinum, byssinum, crystallinum, hyacinthinum, bombycinum, onychinum, amethystinum, smaragdinum,* and the like are Greek, they should be short in the penult, as the Greeks make them. Moreover, these are not possessives; for there are only two terminations for possessives in Greek, namely in *cos,* as *grammaticos,* and in *os,* as *uranios,* that is, belonging to heaven. But all the Latin poets make the penult short, and it is not a poetic license, because they all do it in every instance. For what happens rarely and for a reason is to be ascribed to poetic license, but not that which is of common and constant occurrence. Whence Juvenal's *Amethystina convenit illi*. And he likewise says *grandia tolluntur crystallina*, with short penult. Persius also shortens the penult, saying *hyacinthina laena* at the end of the verse, and so do all the poets without exception. Therefore it is not a case of poetic license, but it happens in accordance with natural law. And since in the seventeenth chapter of the second book of Kings the words occur *quasi siccaret ptisanas,* a famous exposition of the words of the Bible, to which all give adherence, tries to prove that the middle syllable of *ptisanas* is long; and the author of this exposition defends himself by a verse of Horace, which reads: *Tu cessas agedum sume hoc ptisanarium oryzae*. But it is an error, for, as can be proved by all authors, only one syllable is elided at the end of a word in meter; and therefore this should be scanned, *hoc ptisanari oryzae*, making the syllable *sa* short and the syllable *na* long. This is clear for another reason, for in all derivatives *a* before *rium* is long, as *contrarium, armarium,* and numberless others of this kind. This rule is observed in the scansion above, but not in the one generally given, *ptisanar oryzae,* requiring the elision of two syllables, because in the latter this syllable *na* is short, as is evident. Therefore of necessity the middle syllable of this word *ptisana* is short and must be grave in accent. Moreover, there is an error in the writing of the word. For in the new Bibles it is given as *tipsanas,* which has no meaning; and therefore the *p* should be placed before the *t,* as in the name of Ptolemy and in many other words. This kind of error occurs over and over again in other words; and we have made such violent changes in the correct rules of accents that there is no help to be found in our teachers; since custom forces all to pronounce badly, as is made clear by a single example in place of the thousands that might be cited. *Butyrum* has a short penult in Latin authors. Hence Statius says in his Achilleid,

Lac tenerum cum melle bibit, butyrumque comedit.

And Macer in his books on Herbs has,

Cum butyro modicoque oleo decocta tumorem.

The Greek also has it short, and the component parts of the word require it. For it is formed from *tyros* and *bos,* and *tyros* is short in the first syllable. The word means milk-food which

Study of Tongues

comes from the cow. But far greater mistakes are made by many, and there is ignorance of the truth in regard to accents on the part of all. But a broader consideration of this matter is required than the limits of the present production permit.

CHAPTER XI

SINCE I have now shown how a knowledge of languages is necessary to the Latins owing to the pure zeal for knowledge, I now wish to state why this should be secured because of the wisdom established for the Church of God, and the commonwealth of the faithful, and the conversion of unbelievers, and the repression of those who cannot be converted. For in four ways is this knowledge necessary to the Church, first on account of the divine Office, because Greek, Hebrew, and Chaldean words are used in the Office, just as they are in Scripture; and we hear many words, which the Scripture does not use, like *agios, atheos, athanatos, iskiros, imas, eleyson, kyrie,* and the like. When, therefore, we are ignorant of the writing and the correct pronunciation and the sense, we shall miss much of truth and devotion in our singing; for we speak like the magpie and the parrot and other brute creatures which imitate human voices, but neither pronounce correctly nor understand what is said. For since we say *alleluia* many times in a year, it is very proper and right that all those who sing throughout the whole Church should know that they are two words, namely *allelu* and *ia*. For *allelu* signifies the same as *laudate* and *ia* denotes *Dominus,* since it is one of the ten names of God, as Jerome writes to Marcella; and in particular it signifies the invisible one, and God is the most invisible of all. Hence it does not designate any one at all who is invisible, but it designates God. In every Mass we say *Osanna,* a word composed of two elements one correct and the other incorrect. For, as Jerome says to Pope Damasus, *osi* is the same as *salvifica,* and *anna* is the interjection of one praying, the first syllable in this case being written with *aleph.* Whence the meaning is the same as *salva deprecor* [save, I pray]. In other cases the first syllable is written with the letter *he* and then denotes a conjunction which the Latin language does not have. And when we salute the glorious

Opus Majus

Virgin saying, *Ave Maria gratia plena, Dominus tecum,* it is very essential for a true and devout understanding that each educated person should know the meaning of the word, and especially so since many thinking that they know make many errors in this matter. There is a Syrian word, *Maron,* signifying Master, from which *Maria* comes; and it is the same as *dominatrix* [mistress], as Jerome says in his interpretations. This meaning especially befits the most blessed Virgin, who is mistress over all the uncleanness of sin that she may drive it from us, and over all diabolic guile and wickedness, because she is the terror of sin and of the demons, like the ordered line of battle of a camp; and not she only, but all who really put their trust in her. This interpretation is most correct and without sophistry. Jerome, however, says in his interpretations that many have thought that *Maria* should be interpreted "she that illumines" or "myrrh of the sea." He does not accept this meaning but says that it should be "star of the sea" or "bitter sea" according to the Hebrew interpretation. And she is rightly called Star of the Sea, that she may direct us to a port of safety; also Bitter Sea, because she lived in absolute poverty and temporal bitterness in this world, and at length a sword passed through her soul in the death of her Son, so that she is an example to us of all patience and a comforter in every adversity in this world. It is necessary for us therefore in all our psalm-singing and prayers to know how rightly to pronounce and understand, and that as regards the proper meaning of words we should know how to frame our petitions devoutly, in order that we may obtain by the goodness of God and the saints and by the merits of the Church what we ask for rightly and devoutly. But we cannot do this without the knowledge of the words in another tongue; and therefore it is very expedient and necessary that we should have this knowledge. The second reason is because a knowledge of languages is necessary to the Church of God on account of the sacraments and consecrations. For intention is necessary to a sacrament, as theologians know. Understanding and knowledge of the thing to be done precede intention. And therefore in every way it would be expedient for the Church that her priests and prelates should know how correctly to pronounce and understand all the words of the

Study of Tongues

Masses and sacraments and consecrations; just as in the beginning the holy and high pontiff, and all the sainted fathers and founders of ecclesiastical orders decided and knew how the mysteries of God consist in words and their meanings. Whence it is not only proper, but expedient and necessary that those who minister the sacraments, beginning with the first exorcisms and purifications and so passing on through baptism and all the sacraments, should know the correct pronunciation and the required sense, to the end that no sacrament may be impaired. But lately throughout the universal Church countless numbers pronounce the words instituted by the Church and do not know what they are saying, nor do they keep the correct pronunciation of the words. This cannot happen without injury to the sacrament. Would that the effect of the sacrament may have full efficacy! And since the Church established these formularies with definite knowledge and all the ancient fathers knew the correct pronunciation and the sense of the words as befitted the sacraments, we have no excuse; but our ignorance is a base and vile one to be excused by no subterfuge. When in the consecrations of Churches letters of another language according to the order of the alphabet are made with the point of the pastoral staff, it is certain that very few make the letters required, as they were originally determined on by the sainted fathers and by the Church, owing to ignorance of the characters of the other language and in particular an error is made in this manner that three figures are made, which in no way ought to be written in the Greek alphabet. For without doubt the figures which are called episemon ϛ, koppa, and the character ϡ are not from the alphabet of the Greeks, nor did the Greeks ever insert them in the order of their letters; but they are figures and marks of numbers. Modern Latins, however, do not bear in mind that the Greeks number with the letters of the alphabet, and that they have inserted to complete their numeration the three figures mentioned above, namely, ϛ ϟ ϡ. But they do this when they count, not when they use the figures as letters and in writing. Hence in writing they never use these three characters, nor do they place them in the order of the alphabet. But the Church determined that letters alone of the alphabet should be written, in the consecration of the Church, and decided to use letters, not the signs of numbers. Therefore it is most improper that erroneous writing of this kind should be practiced throughout the universal Church.

It is a wretched thing that these words $\overline{\text{I H C}}$. $\overline{\text{X P C}}$. are written in Greek letters, and people think that they are Latin, or are in ignorance of the manner in which they are Greek. For without doubt in this word $\overline{\text{I H C}}$. the first letter is *iota,* equivalent to our *j;* the second is *ita,* equivalent to *e* long; the third is *sima,* equivalent to our *s.* And in this word $\overline{\text{X P C}}$. the first is *chi,* equivalent to *ch* aspirated; the second is *ro,* equivalent to our *r;* the third is *sima.*

There is a third reason for the necessity to the Church of God of a knowledge of languages. For many Greeks, Chaldeans, Armenians, Syrians, Arabs, and nations of other tongues are subject to the Church of the Latins, with whom the Church has to arrange many matters, and to give them various directions. But these matters cannot be handled in the right and advantageous way that they should be, unless the Latins have a knowledge of their languages. Of this there is proof in the fact that all the nations mentioned waver in faith and morals, and neglect the orders of the Church pertaining to salvation, because a genuine plea is not addressed to them in their mother tongue. Hence everywhere among such nations there are evil Christians, and the Church is not ruled as it should be.

The fourth cause is due to the progress of the whole Church from the beginning to the end of days. For the Lord says, one jot or one tittle shall in no wise pass from the law, till all be fulfilled. And therefore there is an admirable exposition in the book on the meanings of the Scriptures stating how the individual letters of the Hebrew alphabet had significance respecting the ancient people, and how they show the number of centuries through which the state of that race passed as regards the different periods and ages, in accordance with the special powers and potencies of the letters; and then the progress of the Church of the Latins is shown by the virtues of the Latin letters. A similar examination is made of the Greek Church by means of the letters of the Greek alphabet. In a remarkable examination of this kind the periods of time are distinguished as regards the varying conditions of the Church to the very end, and we learn through how many hundreds of years each change happening to the Church in its history will last. If we should unite to this remarkable examination prophecies and reliable testimonies, we would be able by the grace of God to perceive in advance to our profit those things which the Church shall receive in her prosperity as well as adversity. Therefore nothing would be more useful than an examination in this way of the value of the letters along with other similar examinations. For to secure certainty in such important matters many ways are needed, of which the one at least is not ignoble which employs the letters of the different languages. I cannot sufficiently admire the manner in which this examination was devised, although it may seem to the uninitiated to have a weak basis in the letters of the alphabet, which are the first rudiments of children. But according to the teaching of the Apostle, lesser things are more necessary and are to be accorded greater honor. And as God has chosen the weak to confound the strong, so has supreme power given greater weight to matters which we reckon insignificant than the human mind can grasp. Such is the case in these letters of the three alphabets; whence not without cause the epitaph of the Lord was written in Hebrew, Greek, and Latin, so that we might be taught that the Church redeemed by the cross of Christ must consider the virtues of the threefold alphabet; especially since the Church began among the Hebrews, made progress among the Greeks, and was perfected among the Latins.

Chapter XII

IN the second place, a knowledge of languages is very necessary for directing the commonwealth of the Latins for three reasons. One is the sharing in utilities necessary in commerce and in business, without which the Latins cannot exist, because medicines and all precious things are received from other nations, and hence arises great loss to the Latins, and fraud without limit is practiced on them, because they are ignorant of foreign tongues, however much they may talk through interpreters; for rarely do interpreters suffice for full understanding, and more rarely are they found faithful. A second reason is the securing of justice. For countless injuries are done the Latins by the people of other nations, the sufferers being the clergy as well as the laity, members of religious orders, and friars of the Dominicans and Franciscans who travel owing to the varied interests of the Latins. But owing to their ignorance of languages they cannot plead their cases before judges nor do they secure justice. The third reason is the securing of peace among the princes of other nations and among the Latins that wars may cease. For when formal messages along with letters and documents are drawn up in the respective languages of both sides, very often matters which have been set on foot with great labor and expense come to naught owing to ignorance of a foreign tongue. And not only is it harmful, but very embarrassing when among all the learned men of the Latins prelates and princes do not find a single one who knows how to interpret a letter of Arabic or Greek nor to reply to a message, as is sometimes the case. For example, I learned that Soldanus of Babylonia wrote to my lord, the present king of France, and there was not found in the whole learned body in Paris nor in the whole kingdom of France a man who knew how satisfactorily to explain a letter nor to make the necessary reply to the message. And the lord king marveled greatly at such dense ignorance, and he was very much displeased with the clergy because he found them so ignorant.

Chapter XIII

In the third place, the knowledge of languages is necessary to the Latins for the conversion of unbelievers. For in the hands of the Latins rests the power to convert. And for this reason Jews without number perish among us because no one knows how to preach to them nor to interpret the Scriptures in their tongue, nor to confer with them nor to dispute as to the literal sense, because they have both the true letter and their own ancient expositions according to ————* and of other men of wisdom as much as the literal exposition requires, and in general as much as it requires for the spiritual sense. For the text everywhere sounds the spiritual note of the Messiah whom we call Christ, even as the Hebrews themselves are not ignorant, because they expect that he will come, but are deceived in re-

* Blank space in manuscript.

gard to the time of his advent. O unspeakable loss of souls when with ease countless Jews might be converted! What makes the situation as bad as possible is the fact that the foundation of our faith began with them, and we should bear in mind that they are of the seed of the patriarchs and prophets, and, what is more, from their stock the Lord sprang and the glorious Virgin and the Apostles and innumerable sacred authors have descended from them from the beginning of the Church. Then the Greeks and the Rutheni and many other schismatics likewise grow hardened in error because the truth is not preached to them in their tongue; and the Saracens likewise and the Pagans and the Tartars, and the other unbelievers throughout the whole world. Nor does war avail against them, since the Church is sometimes brought to confusion in the wars of Christians, as often happens beyond sea and especially in the last army, namely, that of the king of France, as all the world knows; and if Christians do conquer other lands, there is no one to defend the lands occupied. Nor are unbelievers converted in this way, but they are slain and sent to hell. The survivors of the wars and their sons are angered more and more against the Christian faith because of those wars, and are infinitely removed from the faith of Christ, and are inflamed to do Christians all possible evils. Hence the Saracens for this reason in many parts of the world cannot be converted; and especially is this the case beyond sea and in Prussia and in the lands bordering on Germany, because the Templars and Hospitallers and Teutonic Knights hinder greatly the conversion of unbelievers, owing to the wars that they are always stirring up and because they wish to have complete sway. For there is no doubt but that all nations of unbelievers beyond Germany would have been converted long since but for the violence of the Teutonic Knights, because the race of pagans was frequently ready to receive the faith in peace after preaching. But the Teutonic Knights are unwilling to keep peace, because they wish to subdue those peoples and reduce them to slavery, and with subtile arguments many years ago deceived the Roman Church. The former fact is known, otherwise I should not state the latter. Moreover, the faith did not enter into this world by force of arms but through the simplicity of preaching, as is clear. And we have frequently heard and we are certain that many, although they were imperfectly acquainted with languages and had weak interpreters, yet made great progress by preaching and converted countless numbers to the Christian faith. Oh, how we should consider this matter and fear lest God may hold the Latins responsible because they are neglecting the languages so that in this way they neglect the preaching of the faith. For Christians are few, and the whole broad world is occupied by unbelievers; and there is no one to show them the truth.

Chapter XIV

The fourth reason, the repression of those who cannot be converted requires rather the way of wisdom than the labor of war. For the unbelievers always return to their own provinces, as we see beyond the sea and this side of it in Prussia and in the lands of the pagans bordering on Germany and everywhere else; because Christians signed with the cross although sometimes victorious, yet after making a foreign expedition return to their own lands, and the natives remain and multiply. The faith should first be preached by men wise in all knowledge, but who are well versed in languages or have excellent and faithful interpreters. When we learn that some race will obstinately resist we should not only get ready a military expedition, but men of learning should assemble who should subjugate not temporarily nor a part of the unbelievers, but all of them who are in proximity to Christians, so that at least the Holy Land with Jerusalem may always remain in the possession of Christians without fear of its loss in the future. And although many secrets of the sciences and of the mighty works in the arts are needed in this matter, of which I shall make mention later in many places, not only on account of those now living, but because of Antichrist and his followers, yet the power of languages and of the different letters must not be despised. For such great virtue can consist in words that no mortal can trace it out. And at this I wish to hint in many ways, because the matter is difficult and subject to great contradiction. For we see that the words of the sacraments have infinite virtue. And we know that at the command and at the words of the saints from the beginning of the world the laws of nature were changed and elia [*sic*] and other brutes were obedient, and in this way numberless miracles were performed. But the hand of the Lord is not shortened; and we should believe that if on the authority of the Church and with right intention and from desire many true and wise Christians should utter holy words for the propagation of the faith and the destruction of falsehood, that many blessings might result by the grace of God. Oh, how many tyrants and evil men have been confounded at the words of power and convicted rather than through wars! And not only by the words of the saints or of the faithful, but by the words of philosophers have they been so stunned that they were forced to obey the truth. The histories give us definite information in regard to them, and we have seen many of the people who by certain forms of speech have freed many from very great perils. For by two verses containing the names of three Kings of Cologne it happened that ─────* I know a man who when a boy found a man in the fields who had fallen in epilepsy, and wrote those verses and placed them around his neck, and immediately he was cured. He had no return of the disease, until long afterwards his wife, wishing to confuse his mind because of her love for a certain cleric, caused him to be stripped, in order that he might lay aside at least during the time of his bath the amulet† from his neck to protect it from the water. On this being done his infirmity at once seized him in the bath. His wife frightened by the miracle again bound on the amulet and he was cured. Who will venture to put an evil interpretation on this and ascribe it to demons, even as some inexperienced and foolish people have ascribed many things to demons, which frequently happened by the grace of God or by the operation of nature and the power of the excellent arts? For how has any one succeeded in proving to me that the incident related was the work of a demon, since the boy had neither the knowledge nor the wish to deceive. And the woman who wished to deceive not only her husband, but herself through fornication in removing the writing, after beholding the miracle was stirred by piety and bound on again the amulet. I prefer to view the matter reverently with a view to the praise of God's

* Blank space in manuscript.
† Literally, "writing of attestation."

blessings than to condemn with great presumption that which is true. Likewise in Poland and in many districts charms with which to exorcise are made of iron, which is carried in the hands or is walked over. And likewise of the water in which an accused person is placed, a practice of the Church and her priests. The innocent come forth without danger, but the guilty are committed; just as in the old law a woman accused of adultery drinks the consecrated water and was freed if she was innocent, but if guilty her sin was brought to light. But it is certain that the rational soul, which is superior to creatures lower than angels, has in accordance with the rights of its own dignity great power in respect to creatures of lesser worth; just as we see that heavenly bodies, because they are nobler, have power over what is inferior. And any inferior thing that is nobler in virtue can change a thing that is less noble, so that the ignobler things change to their own natures things more noble, as wine intoxicates a man and fire consumes him. But this takes place in so far as wine or fire is nobler; for everything active is nobler than what is passive, as Aristotle states, and it is a fact that, owing to a defect in any creature, one inferior has a certain prerogative which the nobler one lacks. Since therefore the rational soul is without comparison more worthy than the whole animal soul, there is no doubt that it has great power in its works when it is free from spot of sin or when commanded by the grace of God it acts with strong desire and firm intention. But its especial action is the word, and therefore the saints always performed their miracles by pronouncing words. But the rational soul itself knows how to select the time of the chosen constellations for all its works, as the skillful physician selects the proper time for his medicines and blood lettings and other things, as Hippocrates, Galen, Aristotle, Ptolemy, and other authors state. And such is a fact not only in these things, but in all things in which earthly bodies are altered by the virtues of the heavens; and therefore men of wisdom, not only the pure philosophers, but the saints like Moses and others, performed their works under chosen constellations, as I shall show in the proper place, by the locations of which they changed and excited men to many things, without the loss of freedom of the will. Hence they both waged wars advantageously and carried on many great works. And therefore just

Study of Tongues

as they performed their other wonderful works in their appointed times, so also they formed words, which received great virtue from the heavenly constellation itself, and accordingly they accomplished many things through these words. But these matters will depend on what follows, and therefore I pass them over until we come to the opportune place. If, however, other works can receive virtue from the spotless soul, strong desire, firm intention, and celestial virtue, many sages believe that far more has the word power, which is the principal and the first work of the rational soul, and especially so in the three languages consecrated by the divine mysteries, Hebrew, Greek, and Latin. But let us pause here. For these matters cannot be understood as they should without what follows.

From what therefore has been said in regard to languages, it is evident that the Latins suffer a great loss of knowledge owing to their ignorance of them. Hence in this particular they cannot boast of their knowledge, nay, they are far from glorious and they languish with the loss of knowledge in many fields. Since they have paid no attention to this matter, modern Latins of necessity have been forced to bear the loss along with the censure, from both of which all the sainted doctors, philosophers, and sages remained free.

This is the end of this publication.

Any remaining blank pages are for our book binding requirements and are blank on purpose.

To search thousands of interesting publications like this one, please remember to visit our website at:

http://www.kessinger.net

Printed in the United States
108309LV00004B/135/A